READY...SET...PREPARE!

A DISASTER PREPAREDNESS ACTIVITY BOOK

Special Note to Parents and Guardians, Teachers, and Leaders

Remember to learn about the emergency plans that are in place at your child's school, child care facility, or other places where your child stays when not with you. Contact the school principal's office, child care facility, or responsible adult to find out how evacuations and other emergency procedures will be handled while your child is in their care. Also, make sure to **always** keep up-to-date emergency contact information on file at the school or with the adult caring for your child.

Parents and Guardians, Teachers, and Leaders:

Too often, stories about disasters seem to fill our newspapers and news broadcasts. While adults find these incidents both sad and disturbing, they can be terrifying to young children.

How would you and your family cope with a disaster? Would you know what to do or where to go? Maybe you've already experienced a disaster. What would you have done differently?

The reality is that disasters can occur anytime and anywhere. The key to staying safe during a disaster is for everyone to be prepared.

It is especially important to talk to children about disasters and to teach them what to do if a disaster occurs. Not only will this help to calm their fears, but it will also increase the chances that children react safely and confidently during an actual disaster.

This activity book is for use at home and other places like schools and day care centers. It is a tool for children and adults to work together to prepare for a variety of disasters. By completing the activities in the book, children will learn about fires, floods, tornadoes, and other disasters, as well as how to protect themselves. As you guide children through the information and activities, you too will learn about disaster preparedness, and be able to ensure your own safety during times of disaster.

This book is organized to help you work one-on-one with a child, as well as with a class or group, making sure that important safety messages and commonly used disaster terms are understood. Each topic in this book has a fun activity specially created for children. First, be sure to read all the facts about what to do before, during, and after each disaster. Knowing those facts will help children do the activities correctly. The activity book ends with a short game to reinforce the key points.

By working through this activity book with children, creating a family disaster plan, and assembling a disaster supplies kit, everyone will be prepared and know the steps to take if a disaster occurs. It is also very important to practice safety measures with children often, so that they remember what to do in an emergency situation.

The more you and your family know about preparedness, the better the chances are that everyone will be able to stay safe during a disaster. Using the information in this activity book will help you to teach these concepts and to discuss them with children to protect everyone's safety.

For more information, visit the Learn More section in the back of this activity book.
Have fun! Ready . . . set . . . prepare!

Hey Everybody!

I am Mario. This is my friend, Angela! She and I are next-door neighbors. A few months ago, there was a disaster where we live. We were not ready. We did not know what to do. But we were lucky. Bright Shinely and Newser came to help us. Boy, are those two smart! Bright is a real expert on disaster safety. He told us that disasters can happen at any time and in any place. Newser knows all about what to do when disasters happen, too.

Angela and I have learned so much from Bright and Newser. We have asked them to help you learn, too. Now, Bright and Newser will help you, Angela, me, and all of our friends get prepared. Being prepared is being ready! They will tell us what we all need to do before disasters happen and how we can be safe in a disaster. Then, if a disaster ever happens where you live, you will be prepared. Being prepared is the best way to deal with disasters!

This book will tell you all about how to get prepared. Bright and Newser made some fun games just for you! First, make sure you learn the steps about what to do before, during, and after each disaster. Then you will know the answers for the games. Ask an adult to help you read through all the tips from Bright and Newser. Your whole family can learn what to do, and how to stay safe during disasters. You will have lots of fun!

TABLE OF CONTENTS

WORDS TO KNOW

Some words about disasters may be new to you. What are these words? What do they mean? Bright Shinely made a list of words to help you learn about disasters.

Aftershock: An aftershock is a small earthquake that often comes after a big earthquake.

Authorities: They are people who are in charge of a place during a disaster. They keep people safe. They can be police, or firefighters, or teachers.

Dangerous: Something is dangerous when it might hurt a person or destroy something. Playing with matches is dangerous.

Disaster: A disaster is a something that causes lots of damage to people and places. It can be a hurricane or a tornado. It can be a storm or a flood. It can be a fire, or an earthquake, or a blizzard.

Emergency: An emergency is something you do not expect. It is a time when someone could be in danger or could be hurt. It is a time to get help right away.

Evacuate: To evacuate means to leave a place in a quick and organized way. We sometimes evacuate during an emergency. When there is a fire drill at your school, you evacuate the school.

Hypothermia: This is a dangerous illness that can happen if your body gets much colder than normal. Hypothermia can happen if you spend a long time in a very cold place.

Magnitude: The magnitude of an earthquake tells us how much power the earthquake has. A high number like 7.0 means the earthquake is strong. A low number means the earthquake is weak.

Officials: These people hold important jobs in your area. They help carry out the rules we live by.

Plan: A plan is what to do next. A plan can list things to do in an emergency. Or it can be a picture of where things are. A disaster plan has the steps of what to do in all kinds of disasters. A fire escape plan can be a picture of your home that shows you how to get out in case of a fire.

Prepare: Getting prepared means getting ready. Getting prepared for a disaster means you will know what to do and where to go when a disaster happens.

Storm Surge: A storm surge is a large amount of water pushed on to shore by strong winds. A storm surge can be 50 to 100 miles wide. It can be 25 feet high. It can be as high as a two-story home!

Warning: A warning is issued by the National Weather Service over the radio and TV. A warning lets you know that bad weather has been seen where you live or is coming soon. When bad weather is close to your home, you need to take cover or evacuate right away so you can stay safe. Warnings can be about floods, thunderstorms, tornadoes, and hurricanes. A weather warning is more serious than a weather watch.

Watch: A watch is issued by the National Weather Service when bad weather might happen where you live. Watches are issued for floods, thunderstorms, tornadoes, and hurricanes. If they tell you there is a flood watch, it means that a flood might come. Your family needs to be prepared to move to higher ground. Listen to the radio or TV when there is watch so you will know what to do.

PREPARING FOR DISASTER

What does it mean to prepare for a disaster? It means that you find out all you can about disasters. Then you get ready for them.

Being prepared for a disaster is everyone's job. You can take steps to be prepared at home and at school. The first step is to learn about disasters and to make a disaster plan. Here are some ideas to help you get started!

Find out about disasters.

It is important to know about the kinds of disasters that can happen where you live and where you go to school. The best way to learn more is to ask questions.

With an adult, call your local emergency management office or local American Red Cross chapter. You can ask questions like these:

- What kinds of disasters can happen here?
- What can we do to be ready?
- How does our town warn us that a disaster is coming?
- How will I know what to do?
- How will we know when to evacuate?

Ask teachers and principals about the emergency plans at your school or care center.

Look at the Learn More section in the back of this book. You will see web sites to visit. You will see books to read. They can help you get even more prepared.

BE SURE THAT ALL FAMILY MEMBERS KNOW WHEN AND HOW TO DIAL 9-1-1.

Make a plan.

Meet with your whole family to talk about your disaster plan. Be sure to tell them what you have learned about disasters. Tell them how important it is to be prepared! Your family can also meet with your caregivers. Start with these steps to make your family disaster plan.

- **Choose an out-of-town contact.** Ask your parents to choose someone to call in an emergency. This person will be your contact. It is best if your contact lives in a different town. Learn your contact's phone number by heart. Practice dialing it. Know when to call. A disaster might happen when you are not with your family. Then you can call your contact. Tell your contact where you are so your family can find you right away.

- **Decide where to meet with your family.** A disaster can happen when you are not with all of your family,

  o In case of a sudden emergency, like a fire, choose a place right outside your home.
  o In case you cannot go home, choose a meeting place outside your neighborhood.

- **Complete a Family Communications Plan.** How will you contact your family? How will you reach your out-of-town contact? Where will you meet? What are the emergency phone numbers? Post your family communications plan near the phone in your home. Ask your family to make copies of your plan. Each family member can carry it in a wallet or purse.

- **Plan for your pets.** If you evacuate, take your pets with you. Pets are not allowed in emergency shelters for health reasons.

UPDATE YOUR PLAN AT LEAST ONCE A YEAR!

YOUR FAMILY COMMUNICATIONS PLAN

Bright Shinely taught us this: If you have a family communications plan, it will be easy to contact your family or friends in a disaster! Ask an adult to help you fill out this emergency contact form. Cut it out. Ask an adult to hang it where all in your family can see it.

MY FAMILY COMMUNICATIONS PLAN

My Name: _Avery Grace DeLong_

My Address: _80 Grove St., Plantsville, CT, USA_

My Phone Number: _860-426-0668_

My Family
Family work and cell numbers:

Work Number: _1-800-653-6800, 203-272-3150 2350, 860-426-1904_

Cell Number: _80 860-302-6518 (dad), 860-919-3964 (mom)_

Who to call in an Emergency

Emergency Number:

9-1-1 ~~or~~ _____

Name and number of neighbor or relative:

Betsy Camas

Name and number of out-of-town contact:

_____

MY FAMILY COMMUNICATIONS PLAN

More emergency numbers:

Local police station: _____

Local fire department: _____

Poison control: <u>1-800-222-1222</u>

Hospital emergency room: _____

Doctor: _____

Dentist: _____

Pharmacy: _____

Other important numbers:

_____ _____

_____ _____

_____ _____

TAKING CARE OF PETS

Do you have a pet? Bright taught Mario and me that we need to think about our pets in our disaster plans, too. If a disaster strikes, take your pets with you. If you have to evacuate, what are some things that a pet will need?

How much food should you take? What kind? _____

Circle other special items you will need:

Tank   Cage   Leash   Collar   Pet Carrier   Medicine   Toys/Chews

 ID Tag Numbers: _____

 Shot Types and Dates: _____

Emergency Contact Information for Pets

 **Pet Doctor (Vet)**

Name: _____

Address: _____

Phone Number: _____

 Kennel

Name: _____

Address: _____

Phone Number: _____

 **Pet-Loving Friend**

Name: _____

Address: _____

Phone Number: _____

 Nearest Hotel for Guests with Pets

Name: _____

Address: _____

Phone Number: _____

YOUR DISASTER SUPPLIES KIT

During a disaster, you may have to evacuate quickly. You might not have time to gather all the supplies you need. That is why it is important to make a disaster supplies kit. Bright Shinely helped Mario and me make our kit!

Bright Shinely has made a list of some items you can put in your kit. Help your family pack enough food, water and supplies for three days. It must be enough for all in your family.

Bright Shinely made this list of some items to put in your kit!
- Canned or dried foods that will not spoil
- Can opener that turns by hand
- Water (one gallon for each person each day)
- Flashlight
- Radio
- Extra batteries for the flashlight and radio
- First aid kit and handbook
- Soap, toilet paper, toothbrush, and other items to keep you clean
- Extra clothing and blankets
- Forks, spoons, knives, and paper plates
- Eye glasses and medicine
- Whistle
- Copies of IDs and credit cards
- Cash and coins
- A map of the area
- Baby food, bottles, and diapers
- Pet food if you have a pet

If you live in a cold area, you and your family have to think about staying warm! Include these other items in your kit:
- Jackets and coats
- Long pants and long sleeve shirts
- Sturdy shoes or boots
- Hats, mittens, and scarves
- Sleeping bags and warm blankets

UPDATE YOUR KIT AT LEAST ONCE A YEAR!

MAKING A DISASTER SUPPLIES KIT— IT'S YOUR TURN!

The Chen family wants to make a disaster supplies kit! They need to know what items to put in it. Can you help the Chen family? Circle the items they must have in case of a disaster.

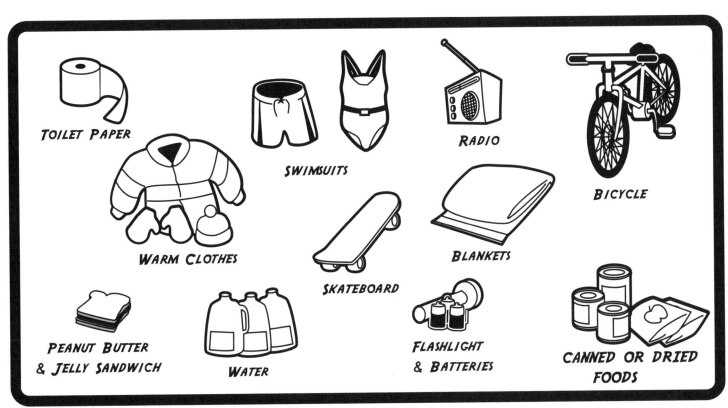

DO YOU HAVE A DISASTER SUPPLIES KIT IN YOUR HOME? MAKE YOUR OWN KIT – THIS IS ONE OF THE FIRST FUN THINGS YOU CAN DO TO GET PREPARED!

PREVENT FIRES & BE SAFE

Fires spread quickly. If a fire breaks out in your home, there is no time. You have no time to pack the toys you love. You have no time to make phone calls. Heat and smoke from fire can be more dangerous than the flames. Breathing the super-hot air can hurt your lungs. If a fire starts, you need to get out of the home right away. Remember that firefighters will come to help you.

Prevent Fires

- If you find matches or a lighter, leave them alone. Go get an adult. Show the adult where you found the matches or lighter. Let the adult put them away.
- If you see a candle burning when no one else is in the room, do not touch it. Find an adult to blow out the candle.
- Keep objects like paper towels and pot holders away from the stove.

Be Safe

Smoke Alarms

- Do you have a smoke alarm on every floor of your home? Is one near the rooms where you sleep? Do you have enough smoke alarms where you live? If not, talk to your family. Ask an adult to install more smoke alarms.
- Remind an adult to test your smoke alarms once a month. Testing smoke alarms will help you know they are working. You will also know what they sound like.
- Your birthday comes once a year. Help your family change the smoke alarm batteries at least once a year, too. Help clean smoke alarms once a month.

Escape Safely

- Walk around in your home to all of the rooms. In each room, find at least TWO escape routes.
- Practice your fire escape plan at least two times every year.
- Practice meeting your family members at your outside meeting place.
- If a fire starts:
  - Get out and stay out.
  - Use your safest escape route – the one away from fire and smoke.
  - If you see a closed door, stop. Do not open it. Feel the door with the back of your hand. If the door is hot, leave it closed. Use a different way out. If the door is not hot, you can open it.
  - Crawl on your hands and knees. Crawl low under smoke. But keep your head up.
  - Meet at your outside meeting place.
  - Tell a family member to go to a friend's home and call 9-1-1.
  - Stay outside. It is only safe to go back inside after the firefighters say it is OK.

IF THERE IS A FIRE, GET OUT FAST. THERE IS NOT ENOUGH TIME TO BRING THE TOYS YOU LOVE. JUST GET OUT AND STAY OUT.

BE SAFE! GET OUT!

Bright Shinely taught us to get out quickly and safely if a fire starts! You can get out fast when you know two escape routes from every room in your home. If one way is blocked by smoke or fire, use your second way out.

Draw a picture of your room in the grid below. Make it show all the windows, doors, and furniture. Draw arrows that point to two safe ways out of your bedroom. Then, find two ways out of all other rooms in your home. Do this with your family.

IF ONE ESCAPE ROUTE IS BLOCKED BY SMOKE OR FIRE, USE YOUR SECOND WAY OUT.

What are some other rooms in your home?

_____

FLOODS

Floods are one of the most common disasters. They can be small – just in your neighborhood. They can be large – in many states at the same time.

All floods are not alike. Some floods grow slowly. They can grow over many days. Others floods grow quickly. They can happen in just a few minutes, even when it is not raining!

You need to know what to do when a flood occurs no matter where you live. Knowing what to do is even more important if you live in a low-lying place, or near water, or near a dam.

Before a Flood

• Learn about the chance of flooding in the places where you live and go to school.
• Know the ways to evacuate from your home and school. Practice these routes.

During a Flood

• Listen to the radio for news and official orders.
• If officials say to evacuate, you may have time. Make sure your home is safe. Ask your parents to bring in outdoor chairs and tables. Ask them to move important items to an upper floor. They need to unplug appliances, and turn off power at the main switches.
• Be aware that flash flooding can occur. If there is a flash flood, move to higher ground right away. Move no matter where you are.
• Turn around – do not drown. Never walk into floodwater. Remind your family to never drive into floodwater.

After a Flood

• Stay away from floodwater. It is very dirty.
• Return home only after authorities say it is safe.
• Throw away any food that touched floodwater. Help your family clean and remove germs from wet items.

WATER, WATER EVERYWHERE

Our friend Sasha needs your help! Last week, there was a lot of rain where she lives. Now the river in her town is rising fast. The river is spilling over its banks. There is flooding near her home. Help Sasha find her route to evacuate. Draw a path through the maze below. Help Sasha and her family get to a safe place!

HIGHER GROUND

LOW VALLEY

FLOODED ROAD

I AM SASHA

GRANDMA'S HOUSE

START

THUNDERSTORMS

All thunderstorms are dangerous. Every thunderstorm has lightning. Strong thunderstorms can also bring heavy rains, high winds, hail, and tornadoes.

The sound of thunder can be very scary. Here are some tips on what to expect. Here is how to stay safe during a thunderstorm.

Before a Thunderstorm
- Learn the signs of a thunderstorm: dark clouds, lightning, and thunder.
- If you know a thunderstorm is coming, stay indoors. Pick something you can play inside.
- Learn the 30/30 rule to keep safe. If you see lightning, start counting to 30. If you hear thunder before you get to 30, go inside. Stay indoors for 30 minutes after the thunder has ended.

During a Thunderstorm
- If you are outside when a storm comes, go inside right away. A car is also a safe place.
- Crouch down, place your hands on your knees, and put your head down.
- Move away from things that lightning can strike. Stay away from trees, fences, phone lines, and power lines. Stay away from things made of metal.
- If you are in the water – such as a swimming pool or lake – get out of the water right away and go inside.
- If you are inside your home, tell your parents to unplug things like stoves, toasters, TVs, and phones.

After a Thunderstorm
- Wait indoors at least 30 minutes after the storm ends. Then it will be safe to go outside.

RAIN, RAIN GO AWAY

Playing outside is not safe when there is rain and lightning. Bright Shinely made this game to help you learn to stay safe in a thunderstorm! Draw a line from each of the word boxes on the left. Make the line go to a picture on the right. Make the line point to the correct way to be safe.

IF I AM OUTSIDE NEAR MY HOME, THEN . . .

IF I AM OUTSIDE AND CANNOT GET INSIDE, THEN . . .

IF I AM IN A POOL OR LAKE, THEN . . .

IF I AM WATCHING TV, THEN . . .

TORNADOES

Tornadoes can happen all over the United States. Sometimes they happen quickly. There may be little or no warning.

Tornadoes have lots of power and can move fast. They are shaped like cones. They can strike the ground with winds up to 200 miles per hour. That is about four times faster than a car! Since tornadoes have so much power and can move very fast, you need to know what to do if a tornado strikes.

Before a Tornado
- Find a safe place in your home where you could go during a tornado. It could be in the basement. It could be in a small room with no windows. The room needs to be on the lowest floor.
- Learn the signs of a tornado: a dark, greenish sky; large hail; dark, low clouds; and loud roaring sounds.

During a Tornado
- Go to the safe place in your home. Make sure you stay away from the windows. If you have time, take your disaster supplies kit.
- If you are in a car, get out right away. Get inside a sturdy building.
- If you are outside and cannot get inside, go to a low ditch. Lie down. Cover your head with your hands.
- If you are in a mobile home or trailer, evacuate to a sturdy building. Most mobile homes and trailers provide no safety, even if tied down.

After a Tornado
- Stay away from any damage you see. Be sure to stay far away from damaged buildings or homes.
- Listen to the radio or TV. You will hear news and advice.

BASEMENTS OR ROOMS WITHOUT WINDOWS ON THE LOWEST FLOOR ARE SAFEST!

WHERE DO I GO DURING A TORNADO?

Bright taught Angela and me some safe places to go in case of a tornado, no matter where we might be. Maya, Mason, Angela, and I are going to practice where to go in case of a tornado. Look at the pictures of us in many places. Draw a line that takes each of us to a safe place. Then find the safe place in your home. Where will you go if a tornado comes? Practice going there with your family.

OUTSIDE NEAR HOME

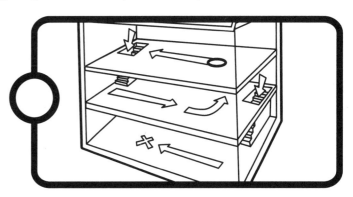

DOWNSTAIRS TO LOWEST FLOOR

OUTSIDE CAMPING

INTO A BUILDING

UPSTAIRS BEDROOM

INSIDE HOME TO LOWEST FLOOR

OUTSIDE IN A CAR

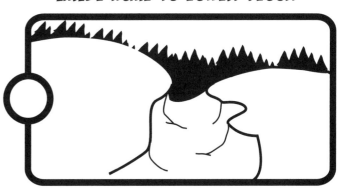

LOW DITCH

HURRICANES

A hurricane is a type of tropical storm that has thunderstorms and strong winds. Hurricanes travel quickly across ocean waters. They cause serious damage to coastlines and nearby places.

A hurricane comes from the ocean. When it gets closer to land, it often brings heavy rains. It also brings strong winds and very high tides (storm surges). Hurricanes can also cause flooding and tornadoes.

Hurricanes travel a long way across the ocean. People have plenty of warning before hurricanes hit land. People have enough time to evacuate to a safe place and stay out of the storm's way. Learn what you can do to be safe if a hurricane comes.

Before a Hurricane
• Learn the way to evacuate with your family.
• Talk about what you would do when you evacuate. Discuss where you would go. Update your disaster supplies kit.
• Remind your parents to bring inside any items that can blow away during a hurricane.

During a Hurricane
• Stay indoors.
• Stay away from water and the shoreline.
• Evacuate if authorities say to do so. Keep in mind that heavy rains could cause roads to flood.
• Take your disaster supplies kit with you when you evacuate.
• Listen to the radio or TV for news.

After a Hurricane
• Return home only after authorities have told you to do so.

EVACUATE TO A SAFE PLACE!

DISASTER SUPPLIES KIT

HURRICANE HAZARD HUNT

When a hurricane is coming, bring things inside. They might blow away in the wind!

Mario and Angela drew this picture for you. Hidden in the picture are items that might blow away during a hurricane. Find these hidden items and circle them!

FIND THESE ITEMS:
BASKETBALL DOG SKATEBOARD ROLLER SKATE
DOLL   BICYCLE   UMBRELLA

WINTER STORMS

Many places in the United States get winter storms every year. Even places that often have mild winters can be surprised by a winter storm! Winter storms can bring heavy snowfall and lots of ice. Winter storms can bring very cold air. Learn how to be safe during a winter storm.

Before a Winter Storm
• Add winter items to your disaster supplies kit: blankets, boots, hats, and mittens.
• Help your parents prepare a car safety kit. Include a bag of sand or kitty litter. Pack a shovel, snow brushes, window scrapers, and blankets.

During a Winter Storm
• If you must play or work in the snow, wear layers of warm clothing.
• Go inside often to get warm. Change your clothes if they are wet.
• If you start to shiver a lot, go inside right away. Go inside fast if you get very tired or turn very pale. Go inside fast if you get numb fingers, or toes, or ear lobes, or nose. You are getting too cold! These could be signs of illness (frostbite or hypothermia) due to the cold.
• Stay home unless you must travel.
• Listen to the radio or TV for weather reports and emergency news.

After a Winter Storm
• The air is still very cold and the wind can blow snow through the air. Dress warmly.
• Sidewalks and streets can be icy and very slippery. When snow blows, it can be hard to see where you are going. Be careful outdoors.

BUNDLE UP!

Alberto wants to go play in the snow. He does not know which clothes to wear. You can help him choose the best clothing for cold weather! Circle the items Alberto needs to wear outside to stay warm.

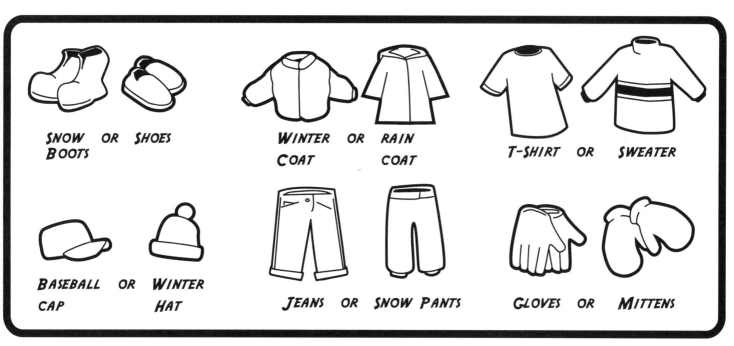

SNOW OR SHOES
BOOTS

WINTER OR RAIN
COAT   COAT

T-SHIRT OR SWEATER

BASEBALL OR WINTER
CAP   HAT

JEANS OR SNOW PANTS

GLOVES OR MITTENS

EARTHQUAKES

An earthquake is the sudden movement of the surface of the Earth. During an earthquake, you may notice a gentle shaking of the ground beneath your feet. You may notice objects wobbling on shelves. You may see hanging plants swaying back and forth. We cannot predict earthquakes – but scientists are working on it!

Earthquakes can be felt over large areas. They often last less than one minute. But, in that short time, they can do lots of damage. If the earthquake occurs in a big city, it may cause many deaths. It may hurt many people. Knowing what to do during an earthquake will help you be safe during this disaster.

Before an Earthquake
• In each room, find a safe place under a sturdy table, desk, or bench. Your safe place can also be against an inside wall or corner, away from things that could fall on you.
• Ask your parents to bolt or strap large items against the wall. Bolt to the walls mirrors, pictures, and tall bookcases. Keep heavy objects on the lower shelves so they do not fall on people.

During an Earthquake
• Drop, cover and hold on.
    • Take cover under a sturdy desk, table, or bench. Cover your face and head with your arms. Hold on.
    • If there is no table or desk near you, take cover along an inside wall or corner of the building. Cover your face and head with your arms. Hold on.
• Stay away from glass, windows, outside doors, and walls. Stay away from things that could fall.
• Stay inside until the shaking stops. Stay inside until it is safe to go outside.
• If you are outside, stay away from buildings, streetlights, and power poles.

After an Earthquake
• Be prepared for aftershocks.
• Open cabinets slowly. Beware of objects that can fall off shelves.
• Stay away from damaged places.

DROP, COVER AND HOLD ON!

HANDLE WITH CARE

Our friend Kailey wants to make her bedroom safer in case there is an earthquake! Can you help her find the things that might be dangerous? Use a blue crayon or pencil. Draw a circle around the items that Kailey can move. Then they will not fall on her. Use a red crayon or pencil. Circle the items that an adult needs to move or fasten. Then the items will not fall on Kailey.

ARE YOU PREPARED?

Congratulations! You have finished the activities in this book. You have shown that you know how to prepare for all kinds of disasters! Great job!

This Bingo game is the last activity in this book. You have learned how to prepare for disasters. Playing the game will help you think about what you learned. There are four Bingo cards so you can play with up to three of your friends.

Getting Ready to Play
• You will need:
    • an adult to help with cutting
    • safety scissors
    • a small paper bag or plastic bowl
    • ten Bingo markers for each player
• Ask an adult to help you cut pages 25, 27 and 29 out of the book.
• Cut apart the ten clues on the Bingo Clues page.
• Cut apart the Bingo cards.
• Make or find Bingo markers for each player. You can use small pieces of paper, pennies, or small pieces of candy. Keep the pieces away from small children and babies.

How to Play
• Choose one player to be the reader.
• Pass out Bingo cards to each of the other players. Give each player 10 markers. The reader does not need a Bingo card.
• Let the reader mix up all the Bingo clues. Let the reader put them into a paper bag or plastic bowl.
• Let the reader pick a clue and read it. Readers, keep the picture covered with your hand. If the players need help, the reader can show them the picture.
• Players with Bingo cards need to find the correct answer on their card. Place a marker on that answer. If you need help with the answer, ask the reader to show you the picture on the back of the clue.
• When you have three squares in a row, be the first to yell "Bingo!" That means you win.
• To play again:
• Pick a new reader.
• Trade Bingo cards.
• Mix-up the clues.
• And….You're Ready….Set…Prepared!

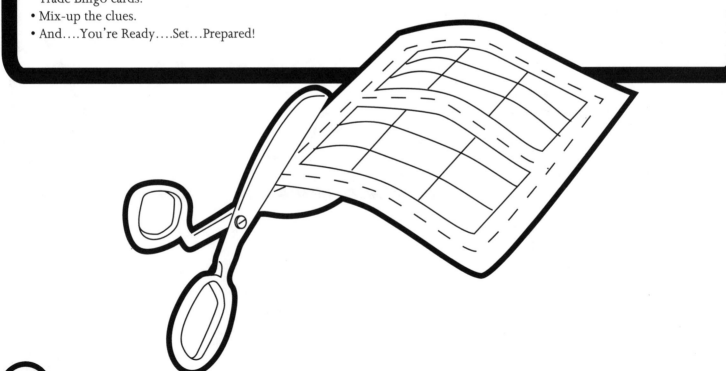

BINGO CLUES - Cut out this page from the book. Then cut apart the ten clues along the dotted lines.

#1
The Kim family chose to gather at the mailbox across the street. What is this called?

#2
Jordan is riding her bike. She notices that the sky is getting dark and cloudy. All of a sudden, she sees a flash of lightning. She starts counting to 30. When she gets to 25, she hears thunder. What must Jordan do?

#3
A tornado warning was just announced in Tonya's neighborhood. Can you help Tonya and her family find a safe room in their home?

#4
Jason is putting things into a duffel bag. He puts in a flashlight, batteries, canned food, bottles of water, and a small radio. What is Jason making?

#5
Kirsten smells smoke and begins to exit the building. At the top of the stairway, she sees flames. She turns around. She knows a second way to get out. It is a good idea to have two of these. What are they?

#6
Caleb and his family just heard some news on the radio. They heard that a big winter storm is heading toward their town. What kinds of items does Caleb need to add to his family's disaster supplies kit?

#7
Dana is walking home from school with her friends. All of a sudden, the sidewalk feels like it is shaking a little bit. She sees a stop sign that is moving back and forth. What is going on?

#8
Jackson and his family left their burning home. They have gathered at their outdoor meeting place. What do they need to do next?

#9
Anita and her mother are driving in a car. All of a sudden, they come to a flooded road. What do they need to do?

#10
Juan lives near the coast with his family and their dog Spanky. The TV news said that a hurricane is coming their way. What can Juan do with Spanky?

BINGO CLUES - Cut out this page from the book and then cut apart the ten clues along the dotted lines.

Go Inside

Outdoor Meeting Place

Disaster Supplies Kit

Room with no Windows

Hats, Mittens, Gloves

Escape Routes

Call 9-1-1

Earthquake

Evacuate with Pets

Turn Around

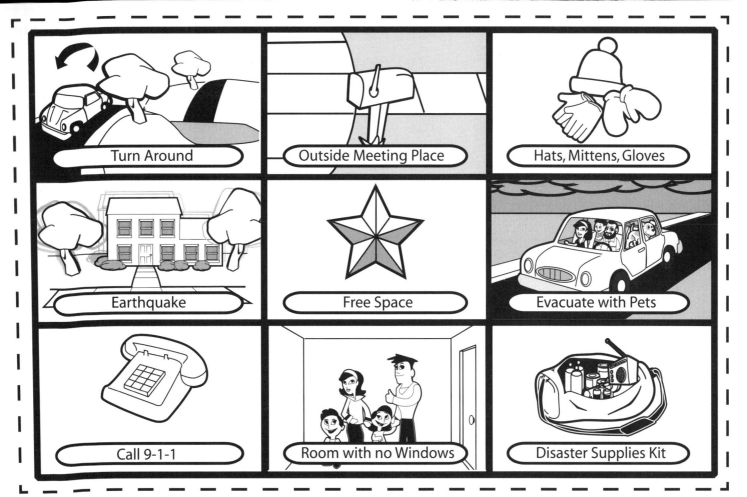

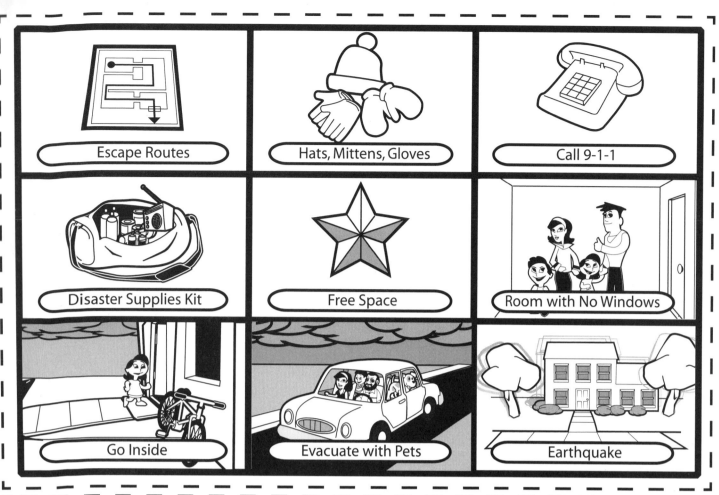

Making a Disaster Supplies Kit – page 9

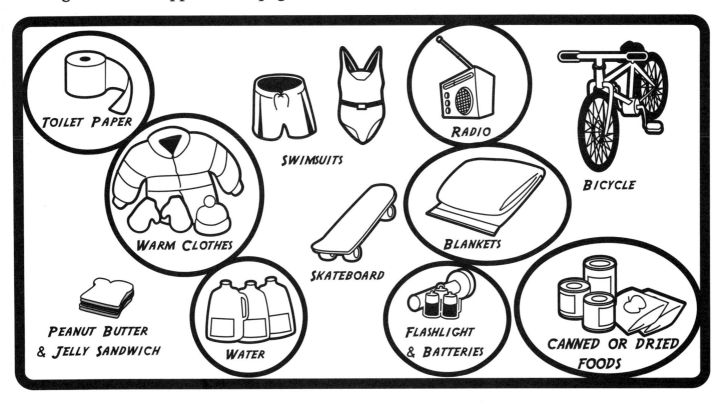

Water, Water Everywhere– page 13

ANSWER KEY

Rain, Rain Go Away
- page 15

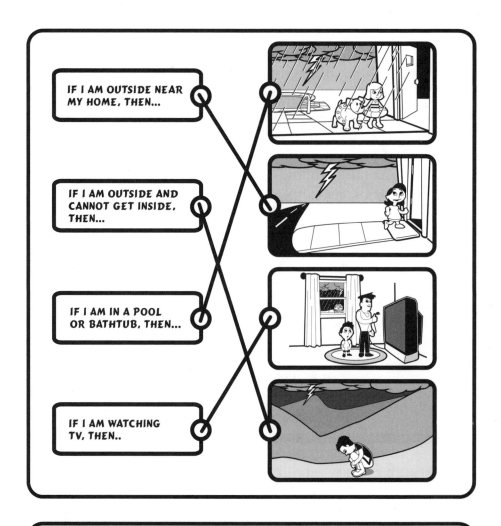

Where Do I Go During a Tornado?
– page 17

Hurricane Hazard Hunt
– page 19

Bundle Up! – page 21

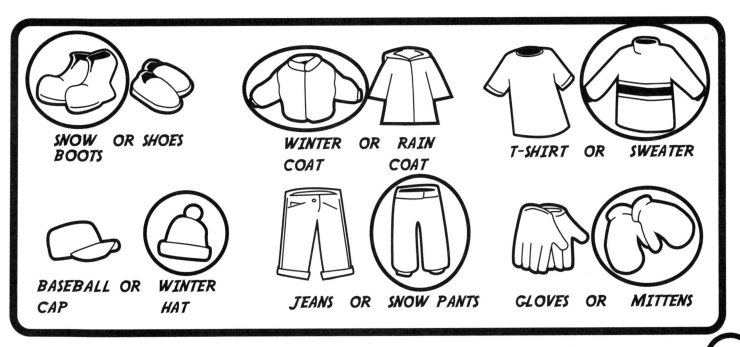

SNOW OR SHOES
BOOTS

WINTER OR RAIN
COAT   COAT

T-SHIRT OR SWEATER

BASEBALL OR WINTER
CAP   HAT

JEANS OR SNOW PANTS

GLOVES OR MITTENS